SEO

Step By Step Beginners Guide to Search Engine Optimization For Web Traffic Growth

Arnold De Vries

1st Edition, January 2017

Table of Contents

Chapter 1: Introduction

So you want more people to come to your website... Big surprise, so do literally all the other websites on the internet! But you know something about 95% of website owners don't have a single clue about: the importance of Google rankings and optimization for those rankings.

And by reading this step-by-step introduction into Search Engine Optimization (SEO), you will have gained a competitive edge that will potentially make you thousands of dollars on the internet.

So pat yourself on the back, because you made a great decision. You just took your first baby steps into the magic world that is SEO: a world where you have the ability to tame the mighty beast that is Google. The Big G is known to change its algorithm recipe a lot though, so it's a good idea to get the basics down and keep learning as much as possible in your journey.

Utilizing this book to help you make sure you are ready to take on your search rankings adventure. You will learn from the beginning what steps you need to take to influence and improve your website for Google. No prior knowledge required. If you do have some knowledge already, then great, you have a head start!

This in-depth guide will help you navigate through the jungle of Anchor text strategies, keyword research, setting up a private blog network and many other useful features to optimize your site. So, starting from nothing, let's get that website going. The following chapters will help you get started with ease.

Chapter 2: The Basics of SEO

In order for visitors to find your website, it is evident that you work with Google's optimization guidelines. In the world of Search Engine Optimization (SEO), there's however much more to be discovered.

Let's start by breaking down the absolute basics of SEO. This chapter will go onto what exactly SEO is, why you need it, and will give an overview of relevant terms that are used in the SEO space.

What is SEO?

Search Engine Optimization (SEO) is, above all, a way to generate traffic to your website. Many people focusing on SEO as an internet marketing strategy seem to forget about this. It is one of many ways to attract targeted traffic to the place you want them the most: your corner of the World Wide Web.

Three major distinctions exist, and depending on the type of website you are building, your path will be greatly determined by these major categories of SEO:

1. **Global SEO:** Often used in congruency with content marketing – ranking your site for broad keywords that are relevant to your site. Global SEO is the opposite of Local SEO.

2. **Affiliate SEO:** Generating traffic for certain product promotions is one of the most lucrative ways to earn money with SEO. Affiliate marketing is a great monetization strategy for your website – This could be product promotion, lead generation or even generating phone calls for clients.

3. **Local SEO:** The act of ranking for geo-sensitive search terms. Or in plain English: physical locations become your keywords. For example, if you have a bakery in downtown Manhattan, you attempt to rank your website about your business for search terms such as: "Manhattan bakery", "New York bread shop", or "NYC Manhattan wholegrain".

Glossary

In the world of SEO's, there's a lot of fancy words floating around. These might confuse beginners, so let's list a few of the most widely used. This is by no means an exhaustive list of terms, but it's helpful to refer to when you're confused what a certain term means:

301 Redirect: A 301 server redirect is the change of a webpage to another page on that same domain (usually the homepage). Used in expired domains to keep the link juice of no longer existing pages.

Adwords: Google service for paid webpage clicks. Essentially used for advertisements on Google for any given search term. The Adwords Keyword Planner tool is a very useful tool for easy and free keyword research.

Algorithm: The lines of code used by programmers to shape the search rankings. We do know the broad outlines of the Google search algorithm, but we can never know it precisely (the only people who know work at Google).

Alt Text: Google's algorithm cannot read images very well. We give alt text keywords to an image in order to let google know the relevance of the contents of the image. Essentially, this is the invisible title for an image only Google can see.

Anchor Text: The exact match text that links to your website. Is explained in detail in a later chapter of this book.

Authority: How powerful Google deems your website or page to be. Often measured using Majestic / Ahrefs / Moz metrics.

Backlinks: The links you are receiving from external websites, which point to a certain page within your own website

Black Hat SEO: The so-called 'dark side' of SEO practices that is not necessarily within the Google Terms of Use. Use at own risk, although often highly effective.

Bounce Rate: How quickly people tend to leave your site. Essentially this is the percentage of visitors on your site that only visit one page and leave very quickly again.

Breadcrumbs: Will show the exact path a visitor of a website has taken. Beneficial to on-page SEO.

Canonical issues: Issues with duplicate content. This means you have multiple webpages on your site with the exact same content – horrible for SEO purposes because Google punishes this hard.

CMS: Content Management System. Basically the software that is used to build a website. The most commonly applied CMS by SEO's is WordPress.

Citation Flow (CF): Majestic SEO metric that indicated the amount of links coming in to a certainly website. Less important than Trust Flow (TF). Optimally you want this to have a >15 value.

Crawler: A bot that quickly analyses all pages on a website.

Duplicate Content: See canonical issues.

Google Dance: The shift in Google ranking positions (See SERP) that is the result of the algorithm used by Google. Usually happens when using PBN sites (which will be explained in a later chapter in this book).

Inbound Links: Links from other websites coming into your website. This is generally regarded as a good thing, especially when the domain that refers to your site has a high authority in Google's eyes.

Indexing / Getting indexed: Google automatically will allow your site to show up in their search engine. This means your page or site is indexed.

Keyword Density: How often the keyword(s) you are targeting are present on a page. Not spamming the keyword is recommended. A few times mentioned is good (especially if it's in the H1-title tags of your article).

Keyword Research: The act of looking for certain words of phrases people are actively looking for on Google. Related to the topic of the website.

Keyword Stuffing: The act of putting as much keywords in your 'Google blurb' (the little text that you see if you search on Google) as possible without making it look unnatural.

Link Building: The act of gathering links to your personal website

Link Exchange: To avoid at all costs. A scheme in which links are exchanged between websites. Often used by directory websites where you have to include a link to the directory in exchange for a link to your site. This will have zero impact on your rankings.

Link Farm: Group of sites all linking to each other. Bad SEO.

Link Juice: The good stuff. If a link is created between website A and B. The power or 'juice' is passed on to that page.

Link Text: See Anchor Text

Long Tail: Keywords which have multiple words attached to them. Very specific search terms.

Meta Tag: HTML in the Head section of a page that gathers certain information. Not visible on the page itself. Is visible to Google's Crawl Engine.

NoFollow Links: These links are ignored by Google for ranking purposes. They occur naturally on all websites and are important to add into the mix of inbound links.

NoIndex Links: Page not indexed at all by Google Crawler. Page will thus never show up in Google at all when a No Index HTML is inserted into the Head of the page's HTML.

Non Reciprocal Link: These types of links have the most value. Basically, if Site B links to your site (Site A), and you do NOT link back to site B, it's a non-reciprocal link.

Organic Link: Not created by SEO, but gained by someone who found your site important or relevant enough to include on their website. Happy days.

Redirect: Certain URL that immediately points to another URL. Will carry over link juice.

Scraping: Using a bot to find expired domains which have high power metrics.

Trust Flow (TF): Majestic SEO metric indicating the power links coming in to a certain domain. More important than Citation Flow (CF). Optimally you want this to have a >13 value.

SERP: Search Engine Results Page. Refers to the position of your page in the Google results page.

Social Bookmarking: Social Media form in which bookmarks are aggregated for public access.

Web 2.0: Websites that encourage user interaction. Examples are Tumblr Blogs, WordPress blogs, etc.

White Hat SEO: The type of SEO that adhere to Google's best practices guidelines. Difficult to pull off compared to black hat SEO. Examples include guest posting, using press releases, or good old-fashioned 'asking another website owner for a link'-method.

Widget: Applications used on webpages for easier use. Often used in WordPress sites.

Why Is SEO Important?

SEO is a way to generate traffic to your website, so the importance simply lies in the fact that 'doing SEO' will give you more people to your site. And if you monetize your website in a clever way, you will indeed be able to get very wealthy from it.

Whilst there are multiple ways to generate traffic to your website, SEO is so lucrative simply because you can decide which terms to rank for. And consequently, how targeted this traffic will be. Finding the perfect terms to rank highly for in Google will absolutely help your online business to grow and flourish.

Should I Only Do SEO?

No. You should not only 'do SEO'. Even the most hardcore evangelists of the SEO world will diversify their traffic generation strategies at some point in time. Only doing SEO is literally throwing your site at the mercy of Google's algorithm. I always advice people to use SEO as a main way to lead organic traffic to their website, but also explore other options. If Google changes their rules on how to rank websites (which they did on multiple occasions in their history), you might potentially lose ALL your website traffic. So it's great advice to also be very active on social media (which in turn will automatically boost your website's SEO rankings, by the way). There's a multitude of other options to explore in order to generate traffic to your website:

- Social media interactions
- Google AdWords
- Facebook advertising
- Offline marketing campaigns
- Network marketing

And this is by no means an exhaustive list of traffic generation options. Traffic generation is an endless fount of resources and possibilities. You will often even see that different traffic generation methods are complementary to each other. However, SEO is certainly one of the most effective ways, if you know what you are doing. Let's dive into the details.

Chapter 3: Keyword Research

Before you even start considering building your website, you should perform a general search of relevant keywords in your particular niche or target market. Following the famous 80/20-principle (where 80% of the results come from 20% of the effort put into something), the act of keyword research is the 20% for achieving SEO results.

Many different methods exist of performing proper keyword research, but I'll explain a very basic and easy (and free) way of finding relevant keywords to target. The tool we will be using for this is called the Google Keyword Planner.

Google Keyword Planner

What better place to check if a keywords gets monthly searches than using Google's data itself? That's why the free to use tool Google Keyword Planner is perfect for keyword research. Admittedly, using the tool is somewhat of a pain sometimes, but at least it's a great free alternative to tools like Long Tail Pro (which have a monthly fee).

The Keyword Planner is actually part of Google AdWords, which is the tool you can use to create paid advertisements on Google's search engine for specific keywords.

Finding the Keyword planner can be complicated because you need a Gmail account to be able to use it, and go through a little maze to find it. Here's the steps:

- Type in 'Google Keyword Planner' in Google
- Click top result
- Log in with your email data
- Register if needed (only once)
- Navigate using the top menu to 'Helpful Tools'
- Click on the keyword planner
- Set your targeting range to your preferred nation you wish to target with your website
- Add your keywords that are somewhat related to your niche in the 'Your Product or Service' box at the top.

The results should look something like the image below. You can choose from Ad group ideas, which are clusters of keywords related to what you entered in your keyword box, or you can look for specific keywords using the tab called 'keyword ideas'. Average monthly searches might no longer be very specific, these have been switched with an estimation.

What Google Keyword Planner should look like

Logic dictates that you wish to select high search volumes with low competition. However, you may also want to go for low volume search keywords with high competition, if there's a buyer intent behind a certain keyword (such as 'product X review' or 'best product X 2017'.

Understanding Keywords

There's a real science behind choosing and understand what keywords to choose for SEO targeting. Whilst most of this will come from simply doing and having experience with what works and what doesn't, here's a few beginner's directions. By following the tips below you will be able to better understand which keywords to choose.

Know your niche

What problem are people trying to solve when they look for your website? What products do these people want to buy or what information would they like to know? Understand the needs of your target audience. Once you have a clear view of what your audience would like to know or have, that's when you can start looking for keywords related to that.

Go for long-tail

It's pretty normal that the search terms you're trying to show up for have a lot of competition. That's why it's a good strategy to adapt your keyword research and go for longer phrases people are typing into the Google search bar. These types of keywords are referred to as 'long-tail keywords'.

And of course, these words need to be specific to your website topic.

Check competitiveness

This goes back to the previous point: don't try to rank for keywords with high competition. Focus on the low competition ones, preferably those with a lot of people that are looking for those keywords. If you have barely any competition, it will be much easier for your new website to show up high in the Google search rankings.

Make a clear overview

When you do keyword research, open up an Excel sheet (or similar) and write down ALL keywords you have found in a list. Mark the most important ones and also write down the competition level, search volume and some additional thoughts about the keywords you found (for example which category they belong to). A clear mind and good research starts with good documentation. Having an overview of your keywords does that for you.

Know What Your Competition Does

A simple strategy I like to use is to actually go out and see what other websites are doing. Obviously, I will only look at the websites that are ranked at the top for the keyword I'd like to be number 1 at with my own website.

There are numerous tools that will allow you to identify the keyword strategies for certain websites, but in my experience the one that has worked best is called SemRush (it's an expensive SEO tool). So if you're serious about this SEO thing I highly recommend you to take a quick peek at what they allow you to do.

You could also just get a quick website analysis by looking at the Sitemap of a competing site, or run Xenu Link Sleuth (a free software tool) to see what links and pages a competing site has got going on. The idea is to 'borrow' the keywords your competitors are using, because these have obviously worked very well to get their site to the top of Google.

Now that you've got an idea of what keywords to target for your new site, it's time to put it into action. We will implement our keywords on our site using what is known as 'on-page SEO'. The details are found in the next chapter.

Chapter 4: On-Page SEO

Now we know what keywords to target, it's time to break down the act of 'doing SEO' on your site. It's not really complicated at all, but you need to know what components to address. In general, SEO is made up out of the following three elements:

- **On-Page SEO:** Using site-relevant keywords in your website pages, so Google can determine the relevance of your site for certain search terms. Determined by (in diminishing importance): page or post titles, URL description keywords, outbound links, links from one page in your website to another, image alt texts, embedded videos, H1-title tags, and relevant content text keywords.

- **Off-Page SEO:** Gathering relevant backlinks to your website, preferably with good anchor text diversification. This means that the links that point to your website have been placed with relevant keywords in them, but not in a manner that makes them look spammy in any way. More about link building and off-page SEO can be found in the next chapter.

- **Social SEO:** This element of SEO is becoming more and more important recently. Having consistent social media activity supports your on- and off-page SEO and will be the secret sauce on top of your ranking efforts. Social SEO means to place links to your site or articles from social media accounts with high power to them. These could be Web 2.0's, or similar.

Optimizing Your Website

The optimization of a website is performed using good on-site SEO. Generally, people who do SEO will be building their site using WordPress, which allows them to install SEO plugins in order to track the on-site SEO performance.

Recommended plugins to track SEO are called 'All-in-One SEO Pack' and 'Yoast SEO'. Both work equally well, but have different systems to them. It's a matter of preference. If you wish to learn more about WordPress and SEO, please consider reading my other book on WordPress website creation. A link to this WordPress book can be found in the final chapter of this book. I highly recommend checking it out, so you will be quickly on your way to get the best performing SEO website.

Forging A Perfect SEO-Optimized Page

Quick disclaimer: I do not promise you this will work for you. I do not promise you this will even work tomorrow. But this is what has worked for me, and what works right now as I write this book. I'm positive at least some of this will continue to be relevant forever, so hopefully this will help in your own SEO optimization process.

Let's try to forge the perfect storm for a basic page on your website. What can you do to optimize it so Google will love it? Let's look at the on-page SEO factors in diminishing relevance. We will take the example of a bakery website that's trying to rank high in Google for the keyword 'Chocolate Donuts'. On the next page you can find what such a page COULD look like. The layout, however, does not matter one single bit for SEO purposes. So do not be afraid to diversify.

The "Perfectly" Optimized Page

(for the example keyword phrase "chocolate donuts")

Page Title: Chocolate Donuts | Mary's Bakery

Meta Description: Mary's Bakery's chocolate donuts are possibly the most delicious, perfectly formed, flawlessly chocolately donuts ever made.

H1 Headline:
Chocolate Donuts from Mary's Bakery

Image Filename:
chocolate-donuts.jpg

Photo of Donuts
(with Alt Attribute):
Chocolate Donuts

Body Text: _____
_____chocolate donuts_____
_____
_____donuts_____
_____
_____
_____
_____chocolate donuts_
_____

_____donuts_____
_____

chocolate_____
_____

_____ chocolate donuts_____
_____
_____chocolate_____
_____
_____
_____
_____chocolate donuts_____
_____

Page URL: http://marysbakery.com/chocolate-donuts

Page title (H1 Headline)

Obviously, your page title should have your exact keyword in it, preferably the very first word(s). Keep the title as short as possible, no keyword stuffing. Also place your exact match keyword title in your Meta Description Title (which happens automatically sometimes). This is the little blurb that you see showing up when you search for websites in Google.

Page URL keyword

In the example, we target chocolate donuts. But our website is called www.marysbakery.com. Make sure that your URL is as short as humanly possible. You can adapt this in the website setting if you're working in WordPress. For our example site, the most ideal situation for SEO purposes is making our page URL: http://marysbakery.com/chocolate-donuts. And nothing more. Then it's perfect if you are targeting chocolate donuts. The key is to place your exact match keyword directly behind your domain URL. And no other symbols, letters, numbers, or unneeded nonsense. Keep it clean.

Meta description

This is one of the most important on-page SEO elements that is technically 'off-page'. Because the Meta description for a page will not show up on your website, but on Google. The description is nothing more than the little blurb of text you see under a page link, when you search for something in Google. The trick is to place our example keyword 'chocolate donuts' at the front of the Meta description title, but also at least once somewhere in the description text. I highly recommend to also include a synonym or similar word to your keyword in your description text, because Google's algorithm will pick up on this. Don't just dump or stuff keywords, but make it a coherent piece of text that someone is eager to click. It's like a tiny sales letter for your page, on Google.

Outbound link to authority site

This is omitted from the example image above, but extremely important for SEO. Add an outbound link to an authority website (a website that is deemed super powerful) which is relevant to your keyword. For example, our chocolate donuts article would at least link one time to a Wikipedia article about 'Chocolate Donuts'. Or a news article on the BBC website about 'chocolate donuts'.

Inbound link to another page on your own site

Interlinking is extremely powerful to help your other webpages on the same website giving each other a boost. Place at least one link to another page on your site in the content of your article. For example, if you have a related article on your site about 'vanilla donuts', link to that with the anchor text 'vanilla donuts'.

Image Alt Attribute(s)

You can at keywords to your on-page images that you embed in your content. These so-called 'alt attributes' can be placed using HTML, or in WordPress by changing the media content. Just place the exact match keyword ONLY ONCE in one of the images (so the alt-attribute will be 'chocolate-donuts' with a dash)

Embedded video (optional)

This will help boost your site even more, but is not necessary all the time. Embed a YouTube video with some traction (a bunch of views and interaction such as likes and comments) that contains your focus keyword. Preferably, this is an exact match keyword.

Body text keywords

Throughout your article, place the exact match keyword, but (very importantly) also variations of this keyword, in your overall text. The example image above shows exactly how to place these keywords throughout your text. It's very important to not force this placement, and simply write your text like a normal human being would. Just make sure you use your keyword at least once or twice. DO NOT overdo it, this will be seen as spam and will seriously harm your SEO for your page. Despite what some so-called experts claim, there is no real rule to when it is 'too much'. Just focus on providing value to your readers and don't spam your keyword, is the takeaway message here.

Relevant Factors Influencing On-Page SEO

There's a multitude of factors that will improve your website's SEO performance in Google's eyes. We will go over them one by one, and give a short explanation. As time progresses, these may become more or less important, as SEO is a dynamic thing, just like the internet itself.

Interlinking

This has already been touched upon, but it is very important to link between relevant pages on your own website quite often. This way, the link power will flow between the pages, making them stronger in the process. Google will see this as a positive thing and will consequently give you better rankings.

Website Speed

It's very important to keep track of the loadings speeds on your website. Logic tells us that better loading speeds of pages will give you better SEO results. Google provides website owners with a simple to use and understand free tool to track what to improve with regards to website speed. You can find the tool here and simply enter your website domain name to get the results:
https://developers.google.com/speed/pagespeed/insights/.

Responsiveness

This basically boils down to the fact if your website design is suitable for mobile users. The internet is increasingly moving towards mobile platforms: smartphones and tablets. The majority of the traffic already comes from these sources and is only projected to grow. No wonder that

Google deems it extremely important that your website design is 'responsive'. If it's not, fix it immediately. Not having a website design suited for mobile or tablet will completely obliterate your ranking results.

Safety

What's relatively new in the SEO space is the need for an SSL-certificate on your website. This is basically only visible in the domain URL – it will show an https://-protocol instead of the regular http:// ones. Having an SSL is beneficial and will be increasingly important as time progresses. Not only for the privacy safety of your visitors, but also for SEO purposes. Your website host is able to give out an SSL-certificate for your site. Sometimes this will cost you a monthly or yearly fee, but in today's internet that's more than worth the investment to get that competitive edge from your competitors.

Website Age & Size

This one is difficult to influence and will come with time. The older and bigger the website, the more authority Google will give to it. As your site gets older it will collect more backlinks and more domain authority. That's also a reason why expired domains are so popular in the SEO space.

Topical Relevance

Having a very specific niche topic to your site, and sticking to that topic throughout your entire site, will be extremely helpful to determine what the site is about, and consequently will help you rank your site for niche keywords in your specific target market. Staying topically relevant and sticking to your topic is thus essential for some good old Google rankings.

Chapter 5: Link Building

Now that we have an overview of what will make the difference in on-page SEO performance, let's look at the invisible stuff: the off-page link building. Historically, the backlinks have always been the most important factor of ranking a website. Google's algorithm has been built on understanding and giving value to backlinks from other websites, in order to determine which results should show up where for which search terms.

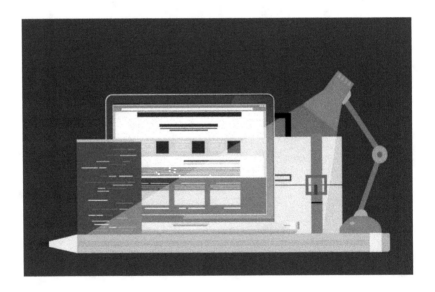

Why Numbers No Longer Matter

Until recently, it has been a common practice to, to say it bluntly, spam the shit out of a website in order to rank it. This no longer works. Over time Google has successfully changed its search algorithm to favor sites that have links pointing to them from websites that are authoritative and are visited by large numbers of people.

It is now common for new websites to rank high with only a few websites who point at them. These must be websites who are both authoritative and are relevant to the site that's getting ranked. You can't really rank a site about dog toys with an adult video site. Well, technically you could, but it's not very effective. It's preferable if you're making a site about dog toys, to get backlinks from already established websites about dogs or pets. The more QUALITY links you gather from other authority sites in your niche, the more likely it is you will show up for keywords in your website's niche.

Finding Quality Backlinks

Now, I can hear you ask: where do you get those links?! And my answer is simple: everywhere they are relevant. If you find an established website in your niche, go ahead and figure out how to get a link from them. Just don't go swapping links with website owners, because that's not beneficial to your SEO performance (anymore). In the world of SEO, we distinguish between the hats we put on when we are building links. We've got the white hat (the 'ethical') methods, and the black hat (the 'unethical' or cheating) methods. If it's a mix of the two, we call that a grey-hat link building method.

All of these methods work equally well, and both categories equally breach Google's Terms of Service. There's simply no way around that. If you are manipulating search results artificially, you are breaking Google's ToS. Google knows this, and Google accepts that SEO exists, despite being against the search results. Interestingly enough, Google's spokespersons have even spoken out about the fact that having SEO is actually beneficial to their overall search results. They also have a version of Google that does not have SEO in it (where SEO activities are filtered out), and the search results are actively worse than the 'real' results we get when searching for stuff in Google.

So do not be afraid when building links: you are breaking Google's terms of service, and Google is completely fine with that. If you do it ethically and will not try to 'break' the search results for your benefit. And yes, Black-Hat SEO can also be done in an ethical manner, believe it or not (this is obviously an opinion, but Black Hat backlinks are widely regarded as a sound method and are accepted among the SEO community).

Now that we've got the mandatory speech about breaking Terms of Service out of the way, let's look at the ways we can actually improve our rankings. Building quality links is what we are after. We do want as much backlinks as possible, but only from credible sources. Spamming sites with backlinks is a thing from the past. In fact, you should try purchasing 10.000 backlinks for $5 from Fiverr and see what it does to your search results. Exactly, you will get banished from the Google rankings. Or more likely, nothing will happen at all. So keep away from the shitty backlinks and start building links to your site manually. It's completely fine to outsource, but for the love of all that is good and holy, please only purchase links that are proven to work for SEO purposes. And never purchase backlinks if you don't know what you're doing yet.

Okay, now I've discouraged you enough to get you back to reality. So, let's look at what we _can_ do to improve our website's visibility. How do we build high quality manual backlinks that will give us good SEO results? Here's what the real SEO's are doing to achieve results.

White-Hat Methods

Guest Posting

This is the most common white-hat method that provides value to your site. You will create an engaging piece of content that is well-written on someone else's website. Preferably, this is an authority in your niche that will give you a powerful backlink!

Guest posting means you have the ability to tap into a new audience on someone else's website that already has traffic. You help build their site by giving them an article that their readers enjoy, and in return you can get one or two backlinks. One will be a branded URL (your website URL – learn more about this in the next chapter of this book), and if possible try to sneak in at least one keyword specific anchor text (again, please refer to the next chapter to understand what this is).

It's very important that you do not link to this article on your own site, because that would nullify the SEO power of it. Google regards backlinks from authority websites that point to your website, but you NOT pointing back to that site, as the most powerful.

Press Releases

A classic way to gather mass backlinks is to do a Press Release. If you have some news or a big launch on your site, put out a press release. Even it if doesn't get picked up, a lot of automatic press release sites will embed the article on their site. This will give you heaps of good backlinks. A sound method to get a lot of backlinks fast. They may not all be that powerful, though. So don't expect a miracle after releasing one press release article.

Organic Shares (Have Quality Content)

It seems so logical, and I encourage any website builder to do this anyways, but organic shares still work magic. Have AMAZING content that is unique and encourages shares. This includes social media shares, but preferably shares from established websites. Having them mention you organically in their articles is the most optimal way to get a bunch of high quality backlinks to your website.

Submitting Links Yourself

Some websites allow you to actually submit a link to your site for nothing in return. Find these sites and go ahead and make a link for yourself! Especially powerful for local SEO citations (see Chapter 7). Most sites that allow you to do this are databases or directory sites. Avoid directory sites that ask you for a link in return like the plague, it will not help you rank that much at all.

Outreach (Asking for a Backlink)

The classic method of asking for a favor. Very important is that you do NOT do link swapping, that will hurt both your site's SEO. Simply notifying a website owner or author about a piece of content on your site will get you a lot of good backlink results. This goes back to making god, high quality content. If it's relevant and share-worthy, a webmaster will be happy to give you a link for free.

Usually, this method works best if sites already have an article about a certain topic that's also on your website. Notify them that you help them improve that article by including a link to a piece of your own content. And boom! Free backlink.

Sneaky tip: Use a software like Xenu Link Sleuth (free to download online) to uncover broken links on relevant websites. If you find one, make a piece of content on exactly what that link was referring to. Notify the webmaster that they have a broken link on their site and that your content can help replace that link. They will almost always be happy to fix it, especially if you explain that having a broken link on their site is bad for their Google rankings (because that's actually the case).

Black-Hat Methods

Private Blog Network (PBN)

The most important black hat SEO method is the creation of a Private blog Network (PBN). This basically means you will go ahead and purchase a whole bunch of powerful expired domain names and create real websites on them that link back to your 'money site' (also known as the site you are trying to rank). Having a PBN is a quick way to generate a boost towards your search engine rankings.

However, it does require a significant time and money investment, thus it is only a good option if you are knowledgeable at what you are doing. You do need to learn from an expert how to build PBN's. Otherwise you will either shoot yourself in the foot building a PBN, or will have no idea where to even begin.

Simple steps you need to take:

- Find niche-relevant expired domains with 13+ Trust Flow and 15+ Citation Flow, at LEAST 10 referring domains, and a clean non-spammy anchor text (use Majestic).
- Register the domain using WhoIS domain protection OR using fake login details (this is why this method is considered 'black hat')
- Get a separate hosting account (for each PBN site) under a fake name and if possible use CloudFlare to diminish your PBN footprint.
- Create your website with as little similarities to each other as possible. Create articles on these powerful domains with backlinks to your 'money site' (the site you are trying to rank).
- Backlinks should have good anchor text (see next chapter) and should only have 3 links maximum per PBN to your money site.

Needless to say, using this method requires some training and management. It will also cost you a lot of money.

Investing in a PBN is, however extremely powerful for ranking purposes if you are doing things correctly. But you NEED training on this, otherwise I guarantee you will not succeed and will get your site penalized by Google.

Reducing your PBN footprint is the core difficulty in having a PBN network, apart from the many hosting companies, alias names, and large monetary investment. The method is strictly forbidden by Google, that's why it is a black hat method. However, I know for a fact pretty much every self-proclaimed SEO expert uses a PBN to some degree. Why? Because it works. And it works fast. If you do it correctly, that is.

Buying Backlinks

Commonplace in SEO, but strictly forbidden by Google. Exchange money for rankings is not only technically forbidden by Google, it can be dangerous. You do not have control over your links, even if they come from someone else's PBN. Good backlinks can be found on marketplaces like Konker.io, or PBN Butler. Fiverr also has a few but they also have extremely terrible ones. You want to look for manual link building. I do not encourage you to buy links, I am just letting you know that this exists. It is strictly forbidden by Google, thus another Black Hat SEO method.

Chapter 6: Anchor Text

One of the most important aspects about understanding off-page SEO, is having an understanding of what anchor text is and how it can help you rank your website. We will go over both topics and hopefully you will understand the concept a bit better.

What is Anchor Text?

We all know what it is, because if you ever browsed the internet you've seen them. Anchor texts are basically those little clickable words in an article, which will bring you to another page or website. We can implement these clickable words using HTML code (or by simply adding a link in your text in WordPress):

ANCHOR TEXT

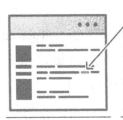

`<p> dolor sit amet, ad per probo partiendo, pro te graeco cotidieque. Nemore quodsi scaeuola te naja, eirmod aliquid epicuri <a href="http://website.com">click here</a> mei cu, fabulas accusam epicurei ex uix. Congue primis posidonium ad est, ne per altera dicunt. Et ius facer temporibus, sea ueniam salutatus interesset. Nonumy inimicus similique an eam, et eum populo uolumus. Mea et ueri lorem inuenire, iudico labitur efficiantur qui no. Tritani aliquid honestatis ne sea, ea cum </p>`

link on a page   link in code

Quite literally, the exact wording which you can click on is what we need for ranking our site in Google. For example, if I have a bakery website, I want an authority website about baking bread to link to my site using the word I want to show up for in Google, let's say: chocolate donuts. So in the ideal situation, I want that authority site about baking to link to my site using a clickable keyword 'chocolate donuts'.

In the image above, the anchor text is 'click here'. If this clickable word world link to your website, your site will actually have a chance of ranking for the keyword 'click here'. So whatever that clickable word is that links to your site, you will have a chance to show up for in Google.

Obviously, you want to show up for low competition keywords in your niche. So that's what you try to achieve when you are interacting with other website owners to get backlinks.

A guest post would ideally include 'chocolate donuts' as clickable word to your site, as well as your website URL. A Private Blog Network (PBN) article would work the same.

There's three types of anchor text:

- **Branded:** This includes your website URL, or a variation of your brand name. At least a significant portion of all the links pointing to your site should contain branded anchor text.

- **Non-branded:** These are the exact match words that we just talked about. Ideally, these should be the keywords you want to show up for in Google. These are basically all anchor texts that are not the website URL variations, or company brand name. You could have other brand names here, which still counts as 'non-branded'. Branded anchor text in SEO terms basically means your website brand name.

- **Misc:** Everything that's not text or URL's. Links within images, terms like 'click here', arrow symbols, other obscure symbols or numbers, anything that's not a search term, URL of your own site, or a variation of the name of your brand or site URL.

How Anchor Text Helps You Rank

Simply put, the website which has the most QUALITY backlinks with keyword specific anchor text will show up first in Google for that specific keyword (or keyword variation). There's however a very thin line between using 'too much' non-branded anchor texts with only 1 keyword in it and using 'exactly the right amount' of them.

As a rule of thumb, you want to do a little dance around your target anchor text, ideally. This is what we refer to as the SEO dance. Basically, it means you build only 2-3 exact match keyword anchor texts to your site, and a LOT (just as much as you need to rank for your keyword) of anchor text that partially contains that targeted keyword, or uses synonyms. This is called anchor text diversification.

Anchor Text Diversification

As an example of an ideal anchor text situation, we take our chocolate donuts ranking. For our example, we assume that all backlinks have equally powerful effect on your site. Then what we would want is 10 sites to have a non-branded anchor text to our site with the following anchor text diversification:

- Chocolate donuts (2x)
- Pure chocolate donut (1x)
- Donut Chocolate flavor (1x)
- Delicious donuts (1x)
- Chocolate baked goodies (1x)

- White choco donut (1x)
- Pure donut choco flavor (1x)
- Nutella organic donut (1x)
- Special chocolatey treats (1x)

And the list could be as creative and big as you would like. The SEO dance basically is that you include a part of the desired keyword, but not the exact keyword in its entirety. We only do this to avoid any trouble with Google. If you're unsure about the anchor text of your own website, go to http://www.majestic.com and check the pie chart of your current state of business. If a lot of non-branded anchor texts pops up, it's time to gather more diverse backlinks as quickly as possible.

Too much of the exact same anchor keywords can very quickly result in a penalty by Google. Google sees something like that very quickly as spamming a keyword. This could result in your site being marked as a spam site, and it could even get de-indexed, which means it will completely be removed from Google search all together. So be aware of this before you start building backlinks, yet do not let it frighten you. If you follow the example, you will most likely be completely safe.

Chapter 7: Local SEO Essentials

A specific subcategory of SEO, but one that's very profitable for local businesses, is called local SEO. Basically, this means that in your keywords you also have included a geographic location, such as a city, region, state, province or even suburb and ZIP code. For these search terms, Google shows maps of relevant companies in the specific area. These maps and the attached companies is called a 'local snack pack'.

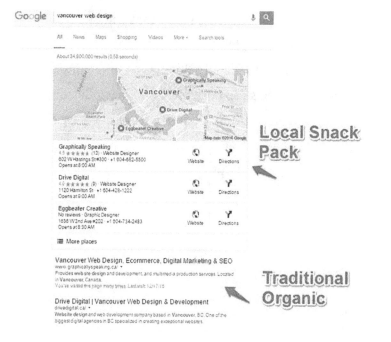

The list of companies always used to be around 7 in total, but has since been reduced to a maximum of three companies. As a company, you really want to be in the top 3 search results for that specific reason. There's a few strategies you should employ to achieve this. This chapter will go over the most relevant factors to rank high for local SEO search terms. This overview is not meant as a guide on local SEO, which could be a completely separate book entirely. We go over three of the most essential things you should do.

Verify Business Ownership

If you haven't done so already, verify that you own your business over at https://www.google.com/business/. Here you can claim your Google 'My Business'-page. Simply fill in the details as precise as possible, and place relevant keywords in the description. Choosing correct categories and uploading at least 5 good photo's is very important to optimize your page (and optimize your local SEO performance).

Google Reviews

This may seem extremely logical, but there's literally thousands of businesses that aren't even looking at this.

However, having loads of 4 or 5 star Google reviews will drastically improve your ability to show up in the local search results. It's very simple: the business with the most reviews that are positive, wins the local ranking game.

Actively ask your customers to leave reviews when they had a good experience. Offer them discounts, rewards or other benefits to do this. Your investment will be worth it ten times over. Because having good Google results is worth thousands of dollars monthly, if not millions, depending on the business you are in. Do not underestimate the power of local business rankings for your business success. Local SEO is an easy way to make your company visible to targeted, local (!) customers.

Local Citations

Your company is likely to already have a few citations, but there's an opportunity to optimize this even further. Citations are basically mentions of your company website (and social media profiles) in directories such as Yellow Pages, Yelp, and so much more. A full list of category-specific websites to place citations can be found at https://moz.com/learn/local/citations-by-category/. More citations equals higher local rankings, simple.

Chapter 8: Search Engine Optimization Tips

Coming to the final chapters of this short instructional book on search engine optimization, I want to leave you with a few useful tips & tricks that will help you propel your website forward. From experience, these are the key elements that helped me give my own SEO operations a boost. Here they are.

Tip #1: Social Media matters

It's no surprise that social media is an important factor within the rankings of Google. Without social media, our webspace looked completely different. But now that we have things like Facebook and Twitter, it's best to use them to our advantage. And by that I mean, gain backlinks from them, and not waste your time posting cat pictures or nonsensical stuff that won't get your results. Focus on your site, not your Twitter account. And if possible automate these social media systems as much as possible. The key is to use them for backlinks, not to waste your time on!

Tip #2: Go mobile or go bankrupt

In 2017 and beyond, having a responsive website is no longer optional. It is an absolute must. Over 70% of Google's internet traffic comes from mobile devices these days (either tablets or mobile phones), and the numbers are rising every day. Therefore it's only natural that Google adapts to this trend by favoring websites that are mobile friendly.

For the website you wish to rank in Google, you must perform what is known as a 'responsiveness check'. This basically means seeing if your website is fit for the many types of mobile devices out there. The process is extremely simple, copy your website URL and go to: http://responsivedesignchecker.com/. Congrats if your website passed this basic test. If it didn't it's time to contact your web designer for an update to your site. Google will literally throw your site into the search rankings dumpster if you cannot pass this basic test.

Tip #3: Build new sites on high-metrics expired domains

There's a simple reason why the market for buying expired domains is flourishing. The main reason being the metrics that are attached to these expired domain names. Simply visit GoDaddy Auctions and see for yourself for how much some domains go.

Not only will you be able to pick up some cool names, looking out for domains with high domain and page power (which are metrics that are retained when a domain expires) are something to look out for.

Tip #4: Get SSL security for your site

The new safety standard will become ever more important in the upcoming time. For a while now, Google favors websites that have an SSL certificate attached to their site. This will certainly impact your rankings and give you that slight edge over your competition.

An SSL certificate can be easily detected by the "https://"-protocol used on your site. If your website does not display this protocol, your website is not SSL-protected. An SSL-certificate can be purchased (or sometimes even obtained for free) from your website hosting provider. Usually, your host will ask a small monthly or annual fee for having an SSL certificate. A basic SSL "https://"-protocol will suffice for SEO purposes.

Tip #5: Outsource the tedious and repetitive tasks

The only way you can focus on creating the best possible website there is, is to actually go ahead and outsource most of the tedious little tasks that come with performing SEO yourself. This will be the only way for you to scale up your online business and actually get some success.

Time is your most precious resource, and the only thing to replace that is money: use your money as an investment to leverage your time wisely. Again, 20% of your actions will generate 80% of the results. Let the other 80% of work be done by hard workers that you have employed.

Go to an outsourcing website such as Upwork and hire some writers, for example. It's really not that much of a money investment as you would think, and it will free up an amazing amount of time for you to do more important tasks.

Tip #6: Don't get lost in the details

There's many small tasks or manual link building to get lost in when you're doing SEO. Don't fall into the trap of getting lost in the details. As you outsource more and more small tasks, you can free up your time to focus on the content of your site and not so much on the SEO side of things.

Again, 80% of the results are achieved by doing 20% of the work. So choose your tasks, and let others do the time consuming stuff. I cannot stress the importance of this enough. If you want to be successful fast, at least.

Tip #7: Silo structure your website

I highly recommend if you're targeting categories or geo-locations, that you look into a website 'silo-structure'. This means, creating a hierarchy of interlinked webpages on your site. For our baker example, the hierarchy could be:

1. Bakery in Canada
2. Bakery Specialties

3. Donuts
4. Chocolate Donuts
5. Pure Chocolate Donuts

All layers of categories would have their own page, linking to a list of subcategories. This will allow link-power to effectively flow throughout your entire website. The URL structure then could look like the following (when targeting pure chocolate donuts in Canada bakeries):

http://marysbakery.com/canada/bakery-specialties/donuts/chocolate/pure-chocolate/.

Tip #8: Be aware of changes in the algorithm

The internet is always changing, and so will the Google search algorithm. Already there's a trend going on that mobile and social signals will be more and more important. As the internet develops itself, this will continue to change continuously. Do not get discouraged by this fact, but use it to your advantage! Stay ahead of the curve by constantly adapting to the newest trends on the web. Does a new social media platform emerge? Get on it. Will Google focus more and more on topical relevance? Build your links only to sites that are very relevant to your niche, before the new rules kick in. This way you will eventually become the king of the hill, even though you might not be that right now.

Tip #9: Don't put your eggs in one basket

Google is by far the most important player in the search engine world, but there's more than just Google on this planet. Think for example about Microsoft's search engine Bing. Or even Yahoo's search engine AltaVista. People actually use all of these tools to find information on the web, believe it or not. All search engines work in a slightly different manner, so it's a good idea to look into some of the other search engines as well.

Another way to look at this tip is to not have 'just' a single website. Putting all your income risk into a single website is a recipe for disaster, income-wise. Always have more than one site that makes you money if that's your core business and core income strategy. If you find a niche that works, by all means go ahead and dominate the keywords of that particular niche. Make 2, 3 or even 5 websites that are about the exact same topic. If it has proven to make you good money, why not multiple that income? Simply apply the exact same SEO linking strategy too all websites, heck, even give them the same type of content and layout. It's all perfectly fine in Google's eyes. They do not care that much who owns the sites. Google only cares about if the content is good and if people enjoy that content (visitor retention statistics).

Tip #10: Be patient and persistent

Building up your website takes time and effort, there is no doubt about that. Mark your goal and identify the steps needed to get there. Every day, make a list of tasks to do in order to get there. Work off your list every single day and you will have certain success. No website is going to skyrocket in a week or even in a month. If you cannot see results, it means you need to keep building content and keep building quality backlinks to your website. There's no hack to becoming successful.

Tip #11: Look beyond just SEO

SEO is just one strategy to generate traffic to your website. Using this together with a sound social media presence will likely propel your site even further into the top of Google. Knowing that paid traffic can also give your site a good boost, especially when you're running some type of campaign, is important within your success story. Don't be afraid to implement strategies beyond SEO, even if it is your main, number one strategy for traffic generation.

It might seem silly to invest in Google AdWords advertising when you are trying to put effort and money into organic search, but it will be worth it in the shorter term, or for related keywords that you do not yet rank for. And Facebook users will not see your Google results, so by all means go ahead and specialize yourself in Facebook Advertisements. More sources of traffic means more prospects that are willing to buy from you, and in the end will result in an increased income level for your websites.

Chapter 9: Parting Words

It will take time and a lot of effort to create a good SEO performance for your site. There's a lot to it, but do not get overwhelmed or discouraged by what you have learned in this short guidebook. Whilst it will help to implement all of this into your website(s), it's certainly not always required to do it absolutely perfectly.

The thing is, your direct competition for the search terms you are trying to rank for is facing the same challenges. And no single site or SEO performance is perfect. So you don't have to be perfect in your SEO either. Set your goal to beat your competition's performance, do not set your goal to be perfect in SEO. Becoming number 1 in Google means to be better than the rest, it absolutely does not mean you need to be perfect in applying all the SEO rules and tricks. Always remember this when you are into SEO rankings. Hopefully, this short guidebook has given you some more in-depth insight into the topic, and will lead you on a path towards a successful, SEO-optimized website. A path that will not be without obstacles, but certainly a path that will be worthwhile, and in the end will be very profitable indeed.

If you are unsure how to start with SEO effectively, I highly recommend you to create a WordPress-based website. There's heaps of very effective tools for this website building framework that will propel your site building efforts forward much faster. I speak from experience when I say that ALL people that have SEO businesses prefer WordPress sites, for their ease of use. Lucky for you, I wrote a great instructional book on how to get started using WordPress. You can find the book by searching 'WordPress + Arnold De Vries on the Amazon Book Store.:

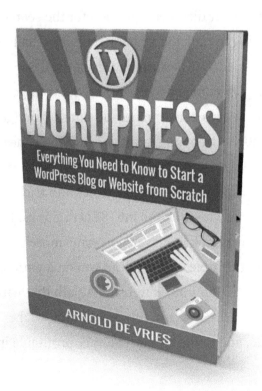

I hope the WordPress book will help you in your SEO journey, just as learning about WordPress sites once helped my SEO business. Hopefully you are now a little bit more knowledgeable on the topic and will be able to start focusing on ranking your site, and providing the best possible content to your readers. Because, yes, it also matters for SEO purposes how long people will stay on your site.

When you build your site and do SEO, please put your effort into the most important tasks that will bring your result, and outsource what you can afford. All the best in your online journey, and my gratitude for giving me the opportunity to get you on your way with your project!